CLICKING IN CREO:
Making Sense of Selection
and Confounding Mouse
Clicking in Pro/Engineer
and Creo Parametric

Bailey Briscoe Jones

Greetings,

Clicking the mouse in Creo is not like clicking the mouse in other programs. Some clicking sequences for the program are next to impossible to discover by trial and error. So, in these pages I'll focus on how to use the mouse to get done what you want to get done. I hope this book will short-circuit some of the inevitable hours of frustration all of us endure as we learn to tame this powerful program.

Keep on clickin',

Bailey Briscoe Jones

Bailey@brightpd.com
Bright Product Development

Contents

Abbreviations 1
General Button Functions 1
Part Manipulation 2
Selection 3
Modifying Features 4
Query Select 7
Selection Filters 9
Curve Selection 11
Solid Surfaces Selection 15
Sketches 17
Sketches, Manipulating Constraints 22
Query Select, Pick from List 25
Seed and Boundary Selection 28
Intent Edges 31
Intent Surfaces 35
Drawings, Placing Dimensions 38
Drawings, Moving Dimensions and Text 42
Drawings, Decimal Places 44
Drawings, Scale 45
Drawings, BOM Tables and Balloons 46
Drawings, Copy/Paste 48
About the Author 48

The figures in this edition come from Creo Parametric 3.0; the clicking philosophy will be the same for previous versions of Creo and Pro/Engineer.

Abbreviations:

LMB   Left Mouse Button
MMB   Middle Mouse Button (or Scroll Wheel)
RMB   Right Mouse Button

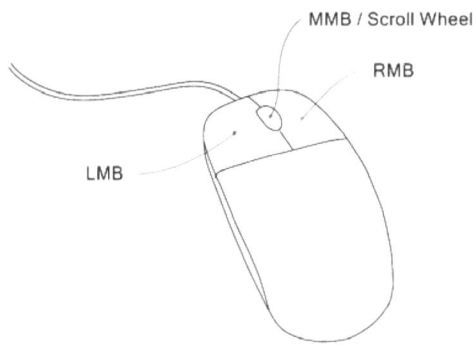

General Button Functions:

The **Left Mouse Button** is used to make selections. To make multiple selections, hold the CTRL key. To clear all selections, click in empty space.

The **Middle Mouse Button** completes a command just like clicking "OK" or clicking the green checkmark. The MMB is also used to place dimensions.   If commands lock up, Creo is likely waiting for a selection from you; use the middle mouse button to complete or escape out of whatever is happening.

The **Right Mouse Button** will bring up a shortcut menu. Oftentimes you will have to *hold down* the RMB instead of simply tapping it. Then, release the button while you hover over the command you want. Occasionally, *tapping* the RMB will bring up an alternate shortcut menu. The RMB can also be used to toggle between choices; more on that later.

<u>Part Manipulation—Zoom, Spin, and Pan:</u>

You can manipulate the part size and orientation in the graphics window by using just the mouse or by using mouse and keyboard combinations.

Mouse only:
Zoom   roll the Scroll Wheel
Pan   roll the Scroll Wheel off to the side of the part
Spin   hold MMB and move the mouse around

Mouse-keyboard combination:
Zoom, fine   hold Shift and roll the Scroll Wheel
Zoom, coarse   hold CTRL and roll the Scroll wheel
Zoom, normal   hold CTRL & MMB, move mouse up, down
Pan   hold shift & MMB, move the mouse around
Rotate, planar hold CTRL & MMB, move mouse right, left

<u>Know where to click during a command:</u>

When you start a command, the areas waiting for a selection are highlighted in red. The highlighted tab is the area that needs your attention first. Also, the prompt at the bottom of the screen indicates what Creo wants you to click. The messages that appear there often help when you get stuck. The red dots indicate other areas where you need to make a selection. Activate that selection by clicking in the box. See the following figure:

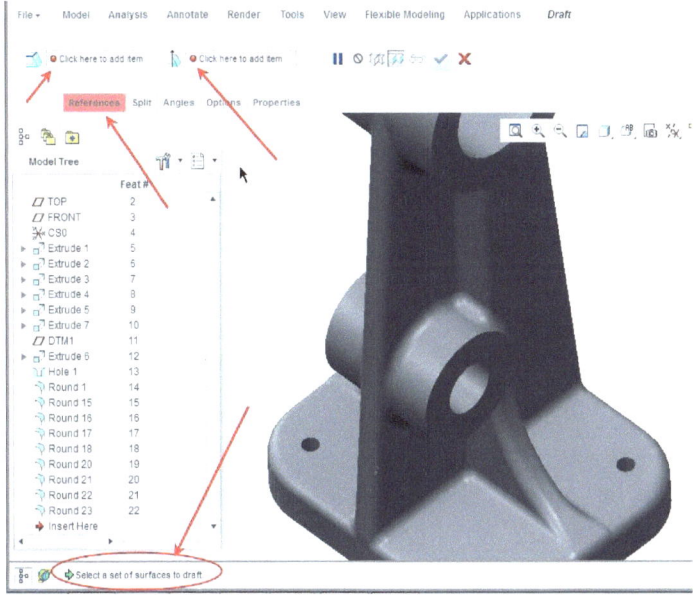

Selection:

Creo has a **Graphics Window** that shows the part geometry and it has a **Model Tree** that keeps a sequential list of every feature of the part. See the following figure:

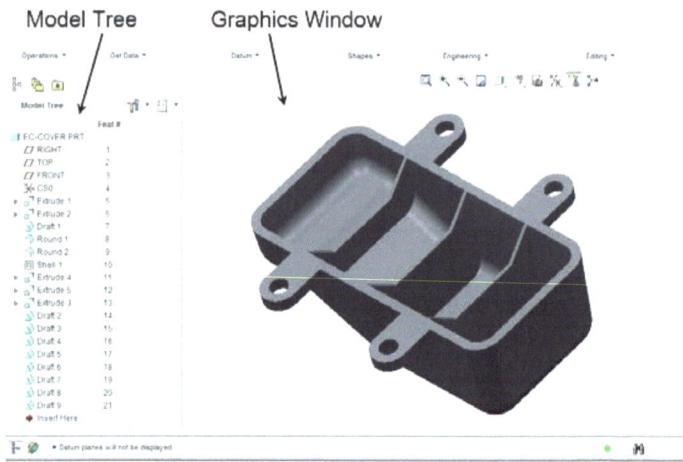

In the Graphics Window, Creo uses what it calls **Preselect** to let you know what you will be clicking on. As you hover over a part in the graphics window, the program will highlight the entity that will be selected if you click the LMB. To select multiple entities, hold the CTRL button as you click the LMB.

Modifying Features—Edit Definition:

Creo keeps a history of every feature you created. You may go back in time and select any feature and modify it. You may select the feature in the Graphics Window, or you may select the feature in the Model Tree. First, click the LMB to select the desired feature.

We want to select the hole in this part. You may select the feature in the Tree as shown here:

Clicking in Creo

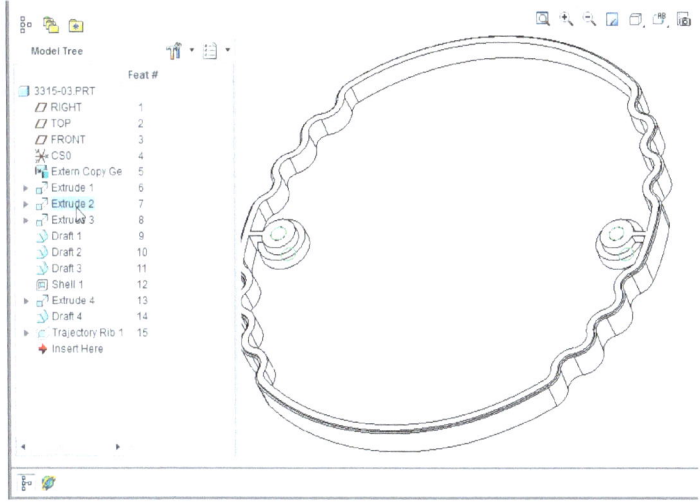

Or, you can select the same thing in the graphics window:

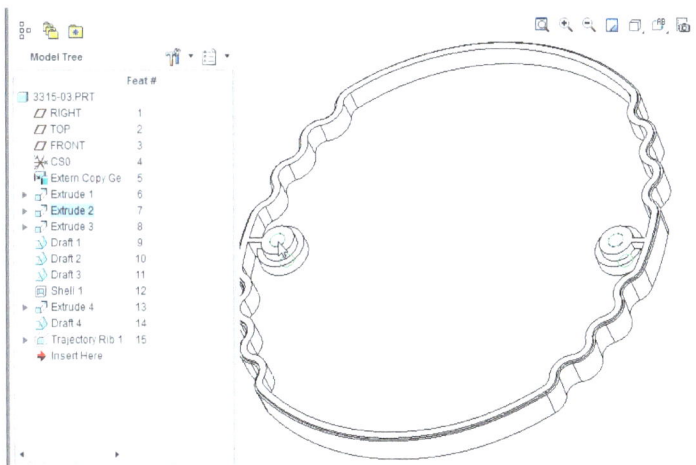

Hold down the RMB and release it over **Edit Definition** to make changes to that feature. Just *tapping* the RMB will not work in the Graphics Window, so hold down the button. See the following figure:

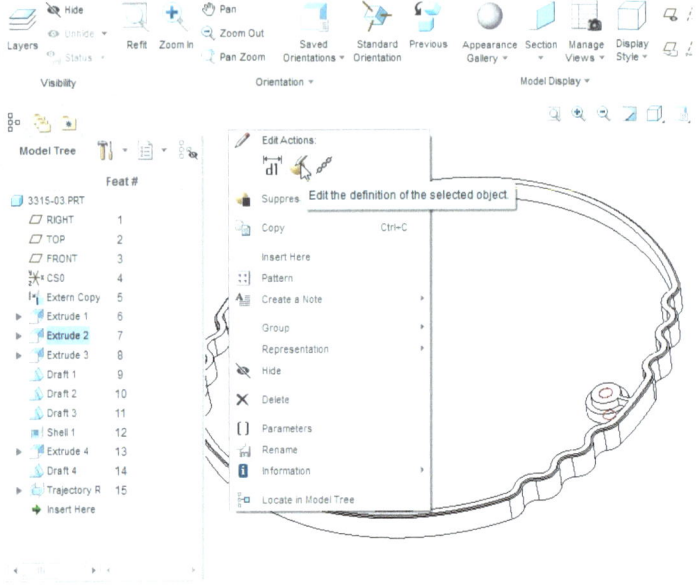

You also have a choice of several other options of what you can do to that feature including suppress, delete and hide.

If you would like to change the sketch (called a Section) that is imbedded in the Extrude feature you can select it by expanding the little triangle in the Model Tree:

Clicking in Creo

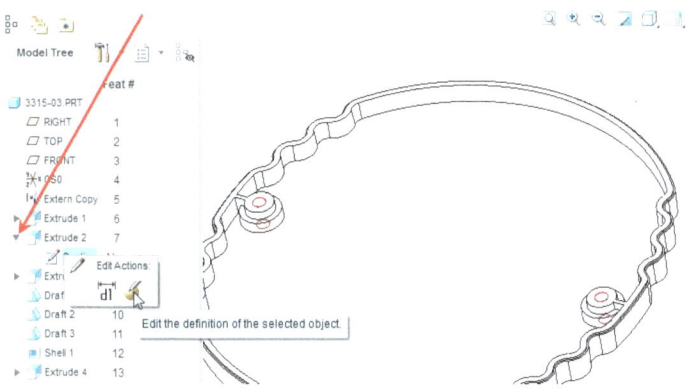

Query Select:

Often, you will be able to zoom in close and click on exactly what you want to click on. Other times this will be impossible. Using **Query Select** allows you to toggle through different options. Hover over the entity that you want to select, and then tap the RMB several times to scroll through your options. When what you want is finally highlighted, you can then select it with the LMB.

LMB Click here and you will select the draft feature:

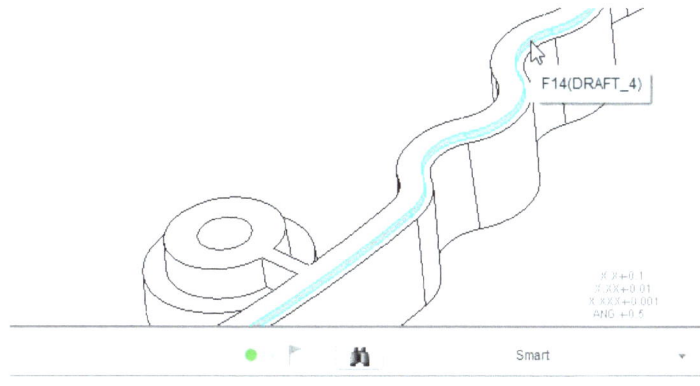

Tap RMB to get another choice:

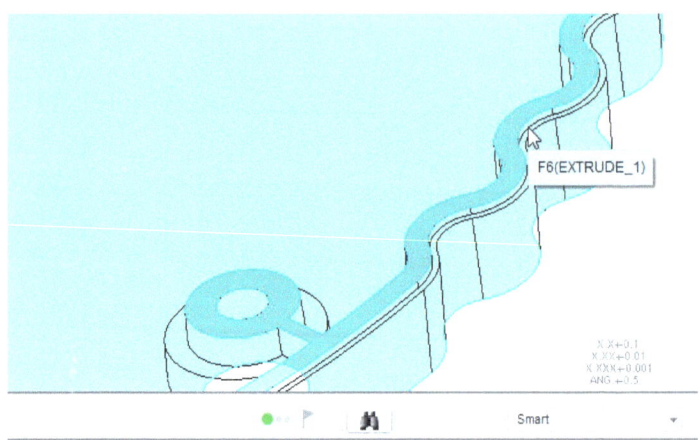

Tap RMB again:

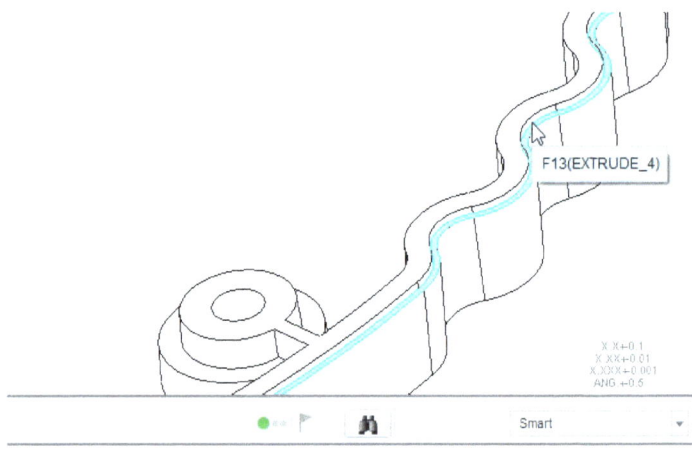

Hit the LMB when what you want to select is highlighted.

With Query Select, you can also pick from a list of items instead of toggling through the choices one by one. *Hold* the RMB instead of tapping to get the **Pick From List** menu. Look at the "Sketches" section of this book for a description of the Pick From List method.

Selection Filters:

The **Selection Filters** are in the bottom right-hand corner of the graphics window. The selection filter lets you click on only a certain kind of entity. "Smart" filter is the default option, and it works in many cases.

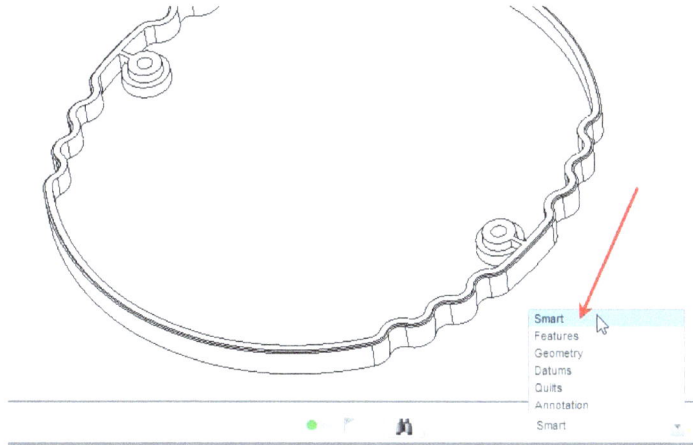

Using "Smart" filter in this area highlights Feature 12, a Shell feature. When you click the LMB, you will be selecting Feature 12. See the following figure:

Clicking in Creo

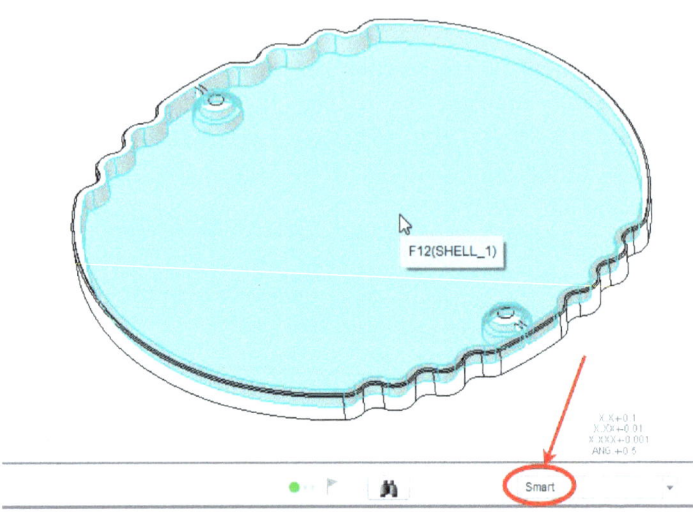

Using the "Feature" filter in this case yields the same result:

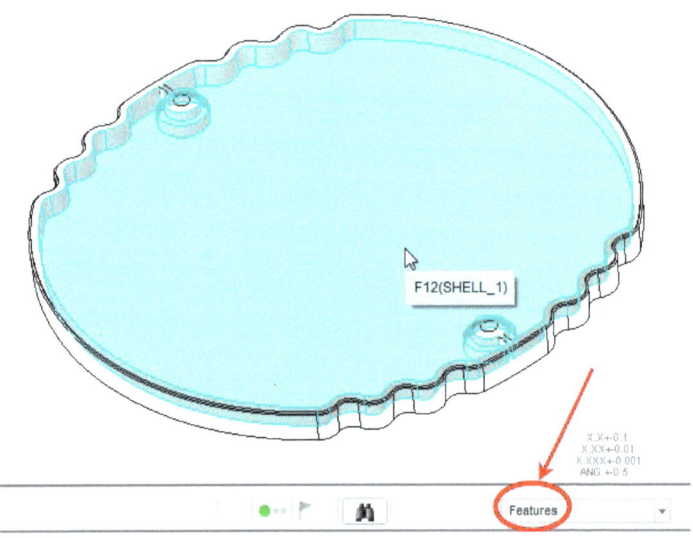

Using the "Geometry" filter allows you to select surfaces, curves, vertices, and edges. In this case, the surface only is highlighted:

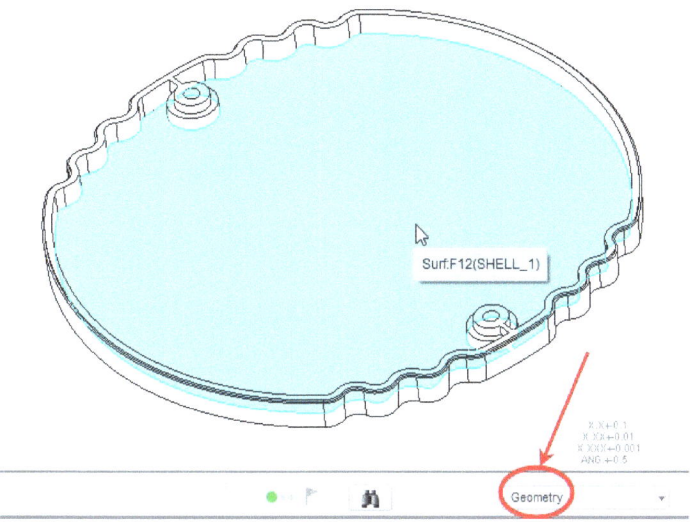

Select a Curve or Curve Chain:

Let's look a little closer at the "Geometry" selection filter. We will use it to select an edge. Notice how only a single segment of the edge gets selected when you click the LMB. See the following figure:

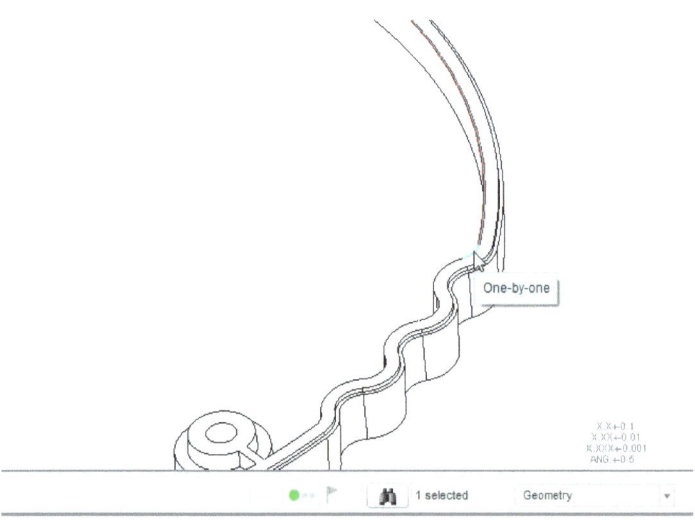

We know that to select multiple *individual* entities, we would hold the CTRL key; but we want to select several entities that behave as one. To do that, hold the *Shift* key and hover over the next area without clicking and this is what you see:

If you clicked there, you would have a single curve entity that was comprised of those two edge segments. But let's say we want to select every bit of the curve that is tangent (a **Tangent Chain**). Mouse over a bit (while still holding *shift*) until the whole Tangent Chain is highlighted:

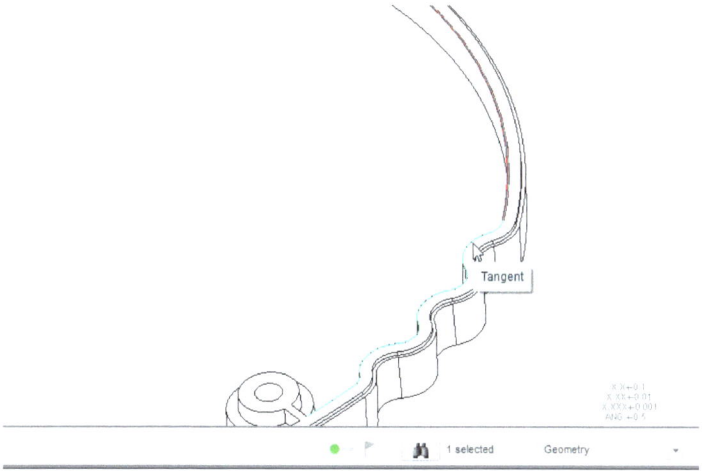

Now click with the LMB and you have selected the entire Tangent Chain. See the following figure:

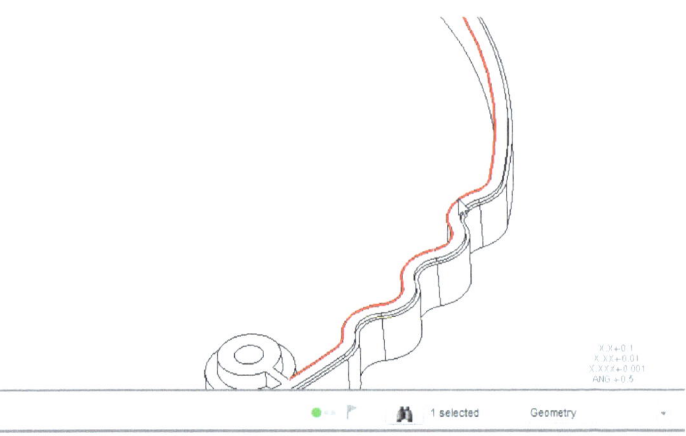

But wait, let's say you wanted the entire curve chain whether it was tangent or not. Before you click the LMB, tap the RMB to toggle through your choices (Query Select) until the entire **Surface Loop** is highlighted.

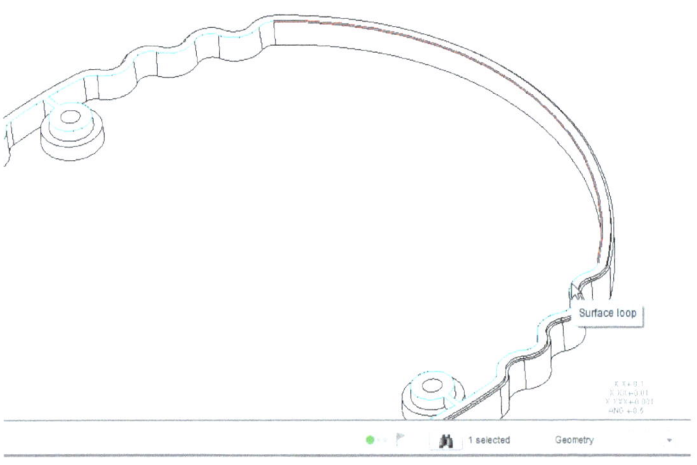

LMB click and then you have selected the Surface Loop:

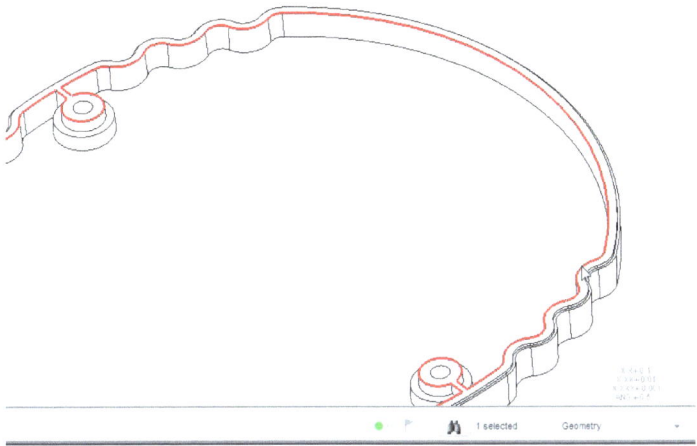

Select all Solid Surfaces:

Sometimes it is necessary to select all the surfaces of a solid geometry. The hard way to do it would be to select each individual geometry surface with the LMB while holding the CTRL key. There is a much quicker way. First, choose the "Geometry" selection filter. Then, select one of the individual geometry surfaces. See the following figure:

Clicking in Creo

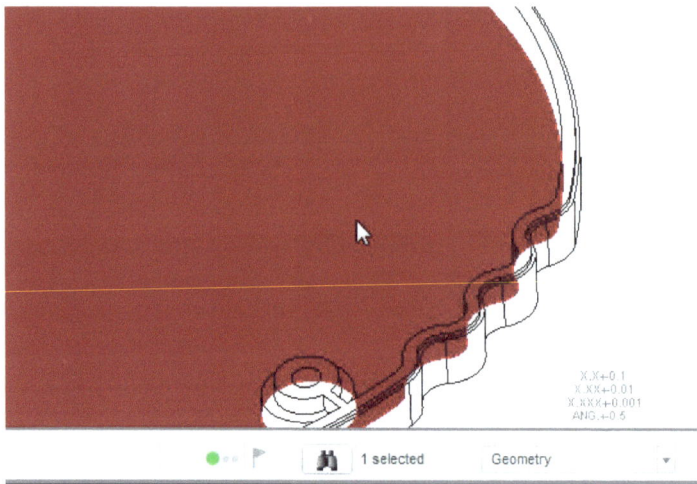

Then hold down the RMB to get some choices and release the button over "**Solid Surfaces**"

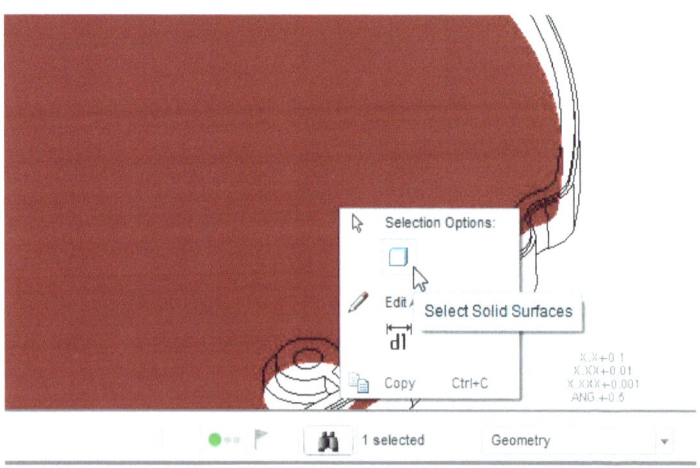

Now you have all the external solid surfaces of the part selected:

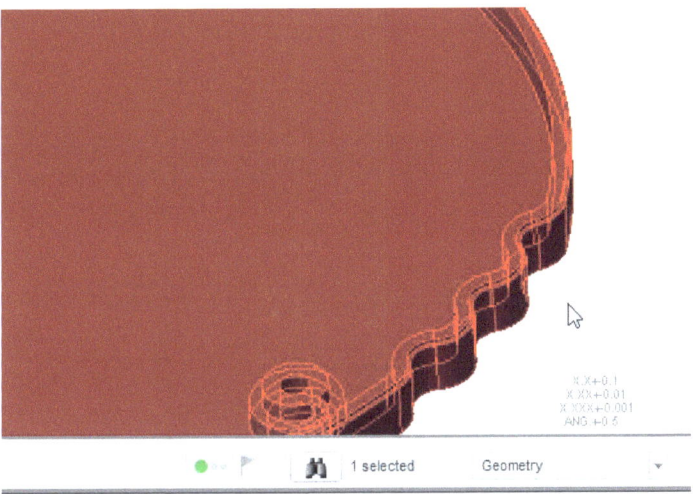

At this point you could copy and paste these surfaces in your model to achieve a stand-alone surface quilt.

Sketches—Picking Entities and Modifying Dimensions:

In order to select sketch entities or select dimensions to modify them, you must use the **Selection Arrow**.

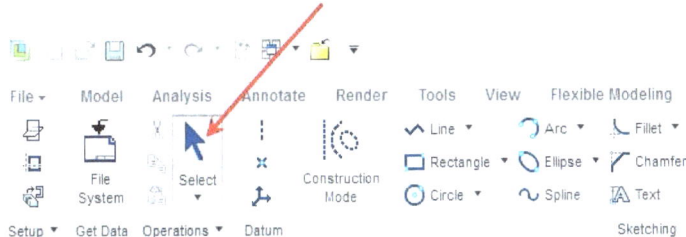

Sketches—Picking References:

In a sketch, references allow you to snap to any part geometry while you are drawing. There are two ways to pick references in a sketch:

1. If you plan ahead, use the **References** button.
2. Or, if you need references on the fly while you are using another drawing command, hold the ALT key temporarily, and then you can pick them in the middle of, say, drawing a line.

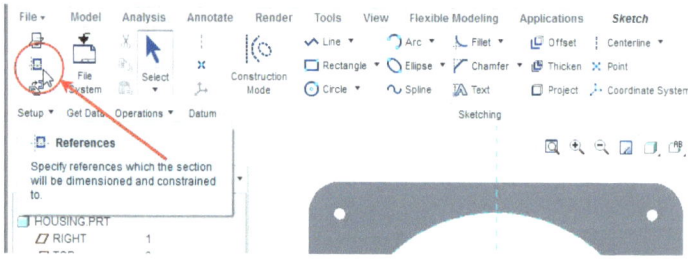

Sketches—Box Select:

While in a sketch you can select many entities at once by drawing a box around the items. First, get the selection arrow:

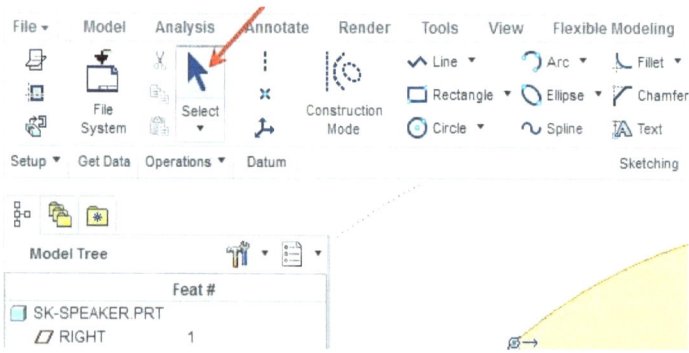

Then, make a box by holding down the LMB and dragging across the screen. Release the button to complete the selection.

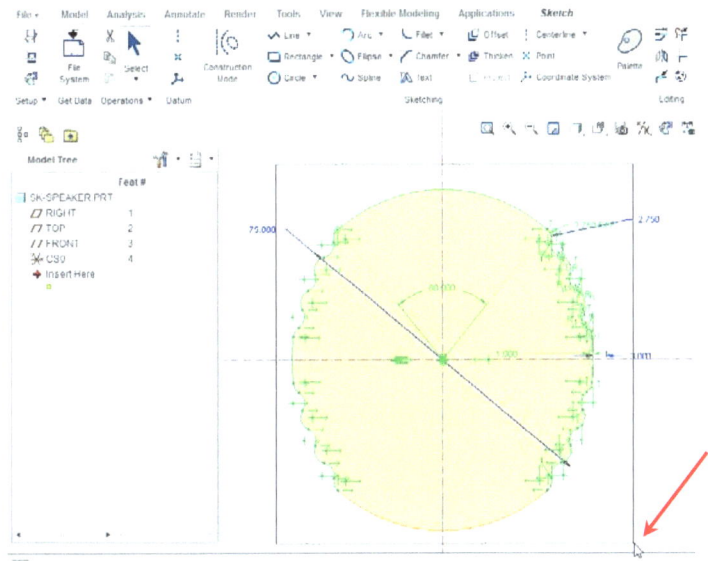

Sketches—Placing Dimensions:

To place dimensions in a sketch you will use a click, click, middle click sequence. For instance, to dimension this angle, LMB click the first line, LMB click the second line, then MMB click to place the dimension. See the following figure:

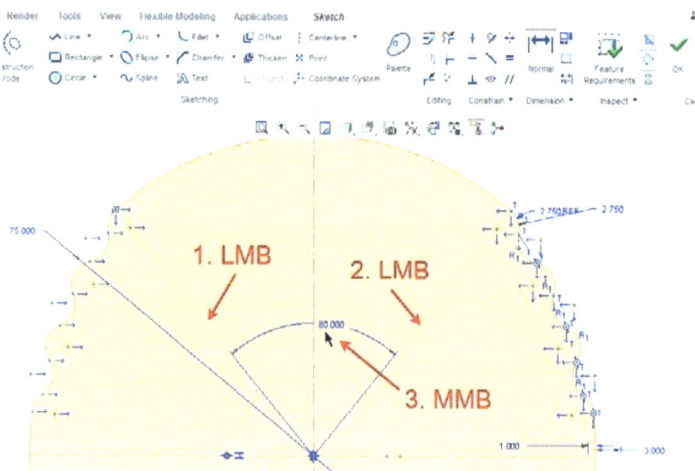

It is very tricky to dimension a diameter or radius until you know the secret mouse clicks. Here are the rules:

1. **Diameter**: *Double* LBM click an arc or circle, then MMB click to place the dimension.

2. **Radius**: *Single* LBM click an arc or circle, then MMB click to place the dimension.

See the following figures:

Clicking in Creo

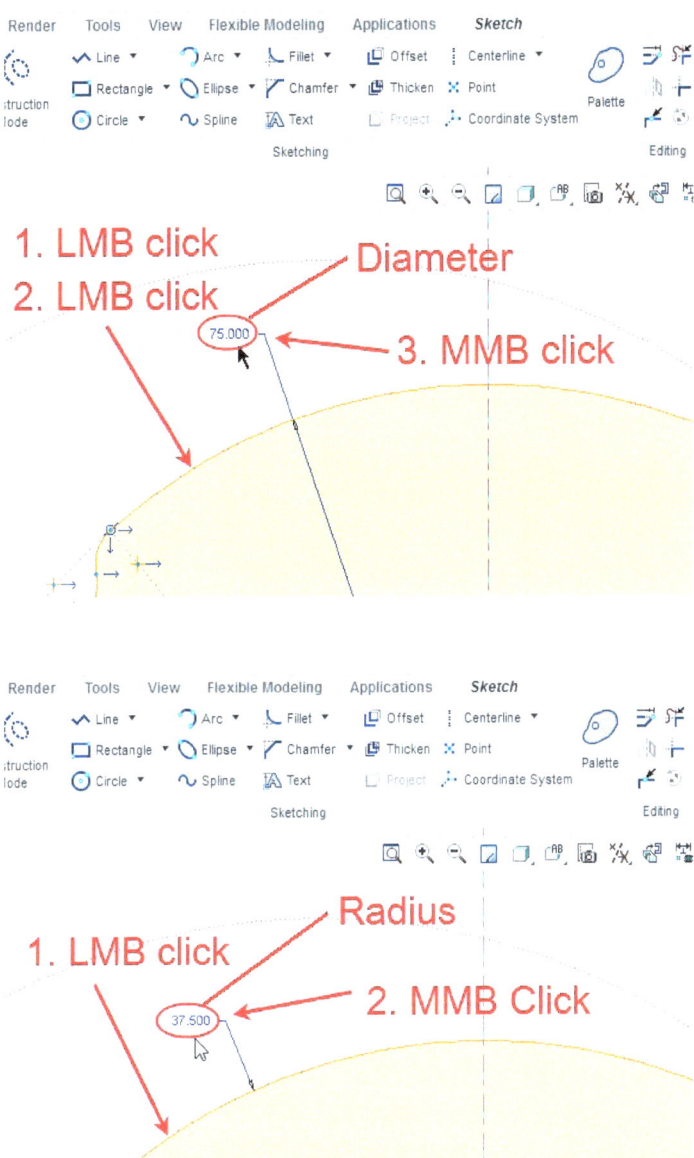

Sketches—Manipulating Constraints:

In a sketch, constraints can force drawing entities to be parallel, vertical, tangent, etc.   As you are sketching, Creo automatically guesses at the constraints that you might want. These are your constraints:

If you want to disable all automatic constraints while you are sketching, hold the Shift key. In other cases, you may need to tell Creo which constraints to keep or abandon. Here is an example where Creo automatically puts a "Coincident" constraint on an arc you are sketching, but you need the end of the arc to be in free space.

These figures show the sketch after you have started the arc, but before you have placed the second endpoint of the arc. You see here, that Creo has put an automatic constraint. If you LMB click now, your arc will be connected to the endpoint of the line. See the following figure:

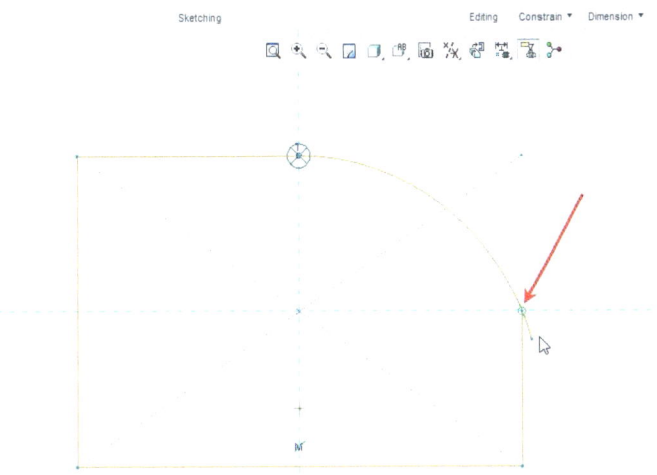

You can lock that constraint in with a RMB click. There is now a circle around the constraint:

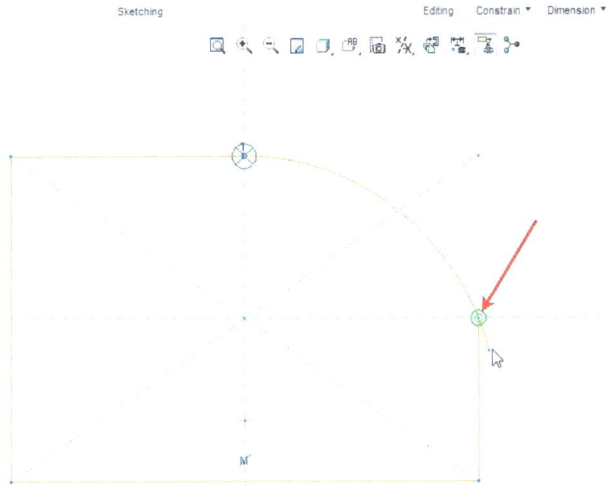

To disable the constraint, RMB click a second time. Now, the constraint is crossed out:

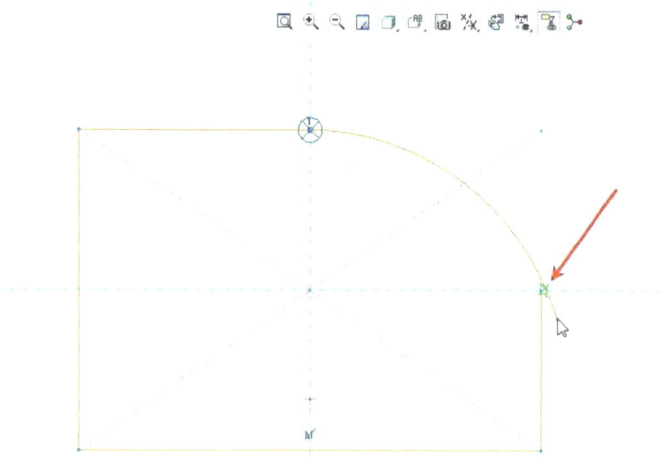

Now when you LMB click, the end of the arc is in free space, just like you want it:

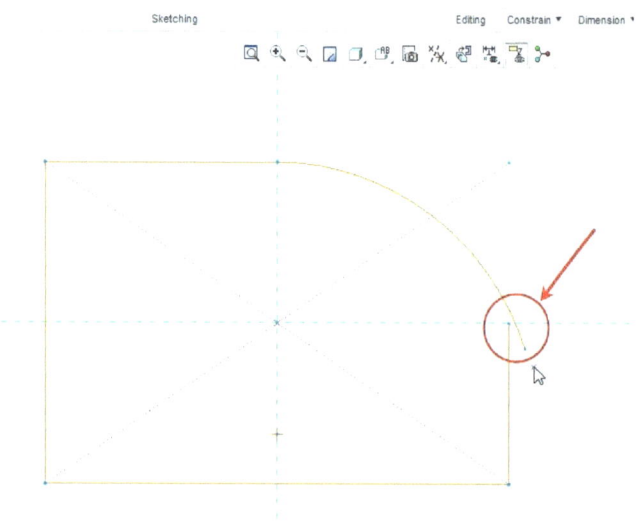

Sketches—Deleting Constraints using **Pick From List**:

Let's look at a way you can use **Query Select** in a sketch to delete constraints. Those little tiny symbols can be next to impossible to click on without it.

Let's say you want to delete this "Coincident Constraint" that shows up as a funny little circle:

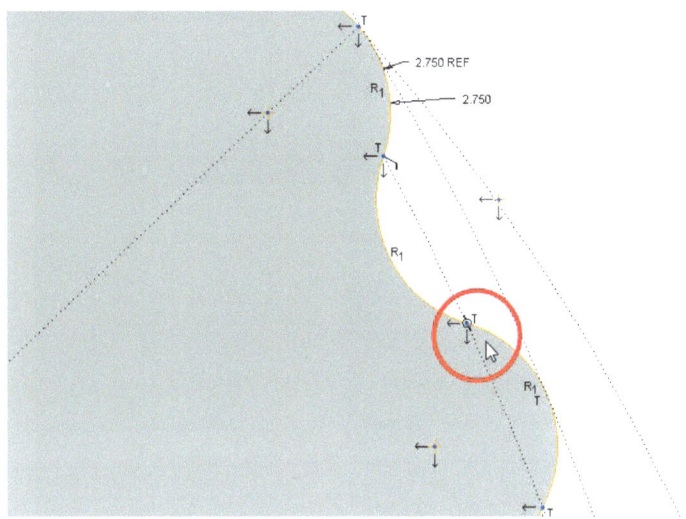

When you hover over it, something else is highlighted instead. See the following figure:

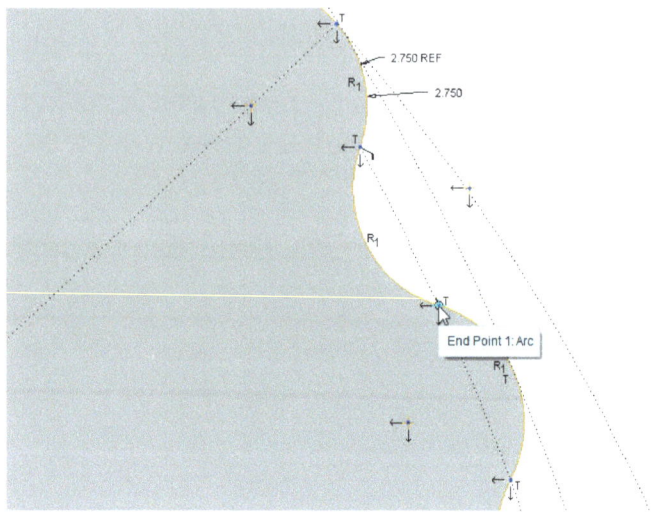

Hold down the RMB and release the button over **Pick From List**:

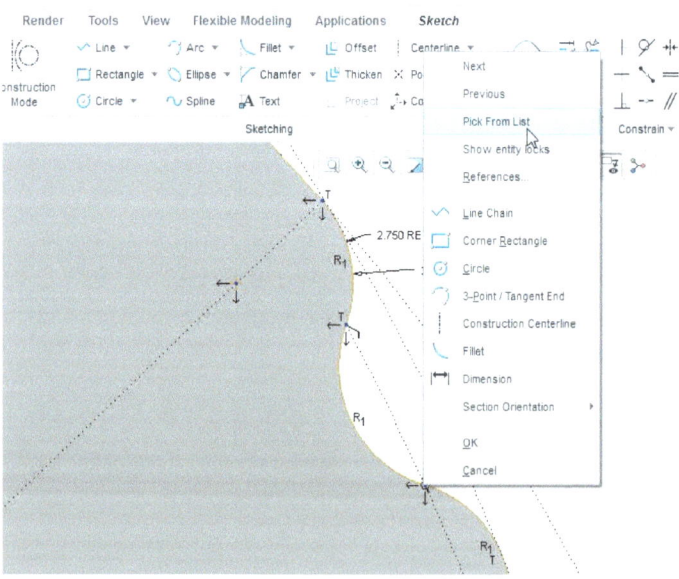

Your selection choices are given in a list and you can select the one you want: Constraint.

Then click "OK" and next you can hit the delete key to get rid of it.

Sketches—MMB as a shortcut:

You can use the MMB in the sketch to save some time. Usually you can click the MMB to complete a command, or if you are in the middle of a command (for instance you have clicked the first endpoint of a line, but decide you don't want to draw a line after all) , you can use the MMB to abort that command. You can also use the MMB to complete the sketch, instead of clicking the green checkmark.

Seed and Boundary Surface Selection:

Seed and Boundary Surface selection allows you to quickly select a set of solid surfaces that are attached to any kind of base geometry. Here, we want to select the surfaces of this fancy post. First, set the Selection Filter to "Geometry".

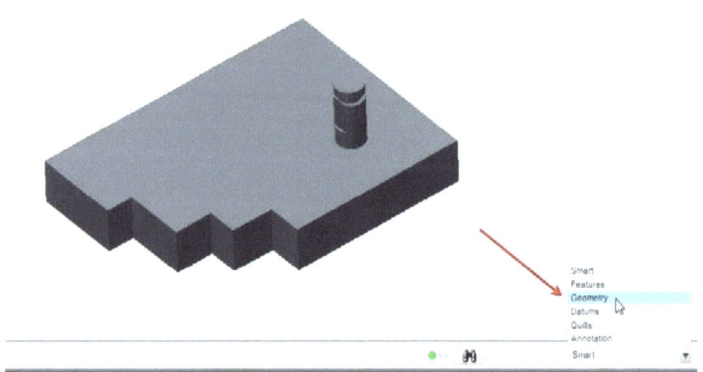

Then, select a surface on the post. This is called the **Seed**.

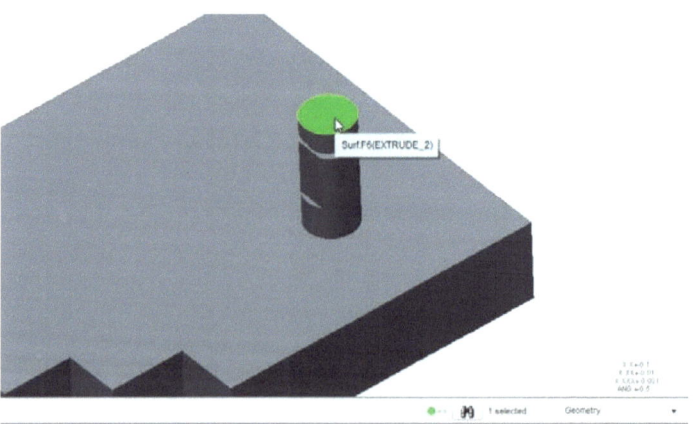

Next, hold Shift, and select the surface that is at the base of the post. This is called the **Boundary**.

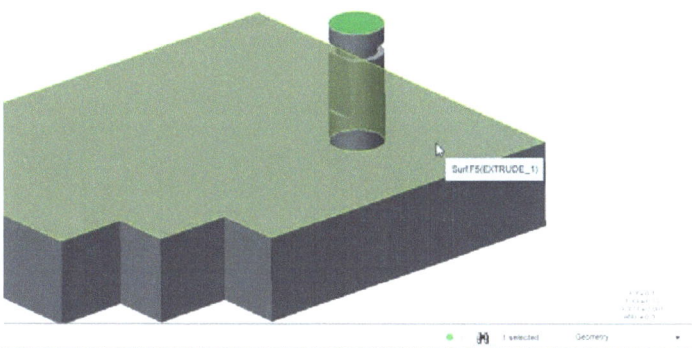

When you release the Shift key, you will see that all the surfaces of the post are highlighted:

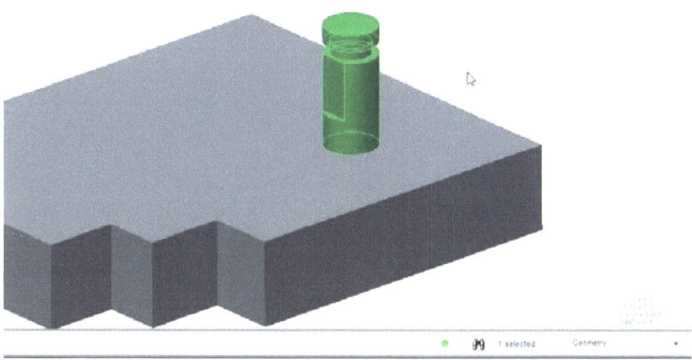

Loop Surface Selection:

You can use a similar method to select a loop of surfaces. In this case, we want to select the band of surfaces around the edge of the base. First, select the top face:

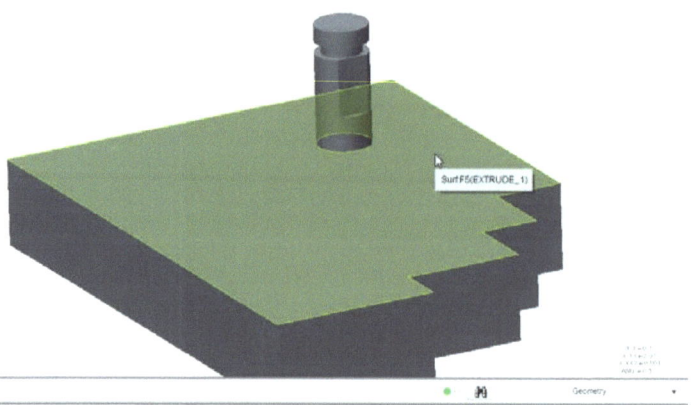

Then, hold the Shift key and select the *edge* around that face:

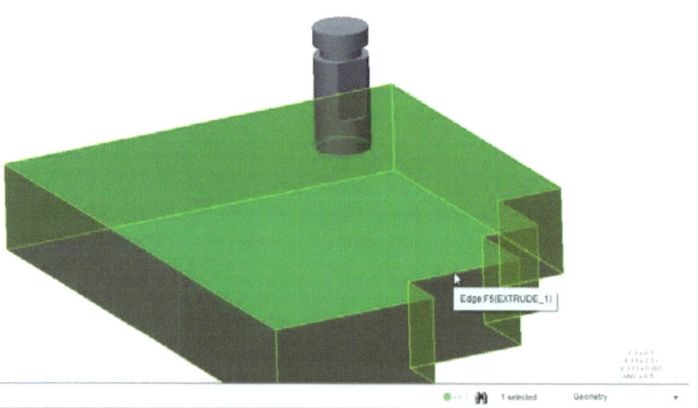

When you release the Shift key, that band of surfaces will be selected:

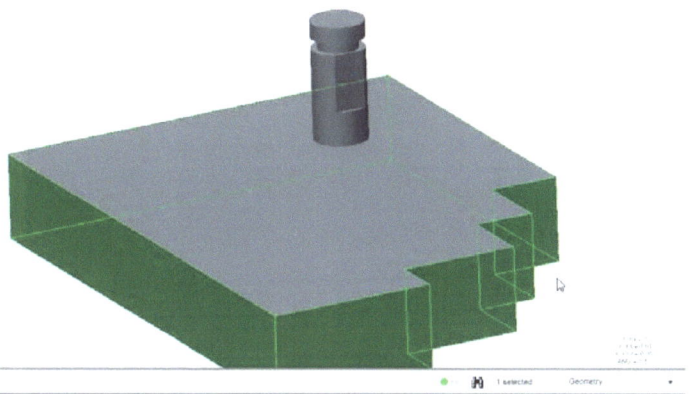

Intent Edges:

Selecting with **Intent Edges** can be a powerful tool. It can do at least two things:
1. Select many similar edges quickly
2. Prevent model reference failures if the geometry changes

Let's say we want to round all the vertical edges of this crown emblem. See the following figure:

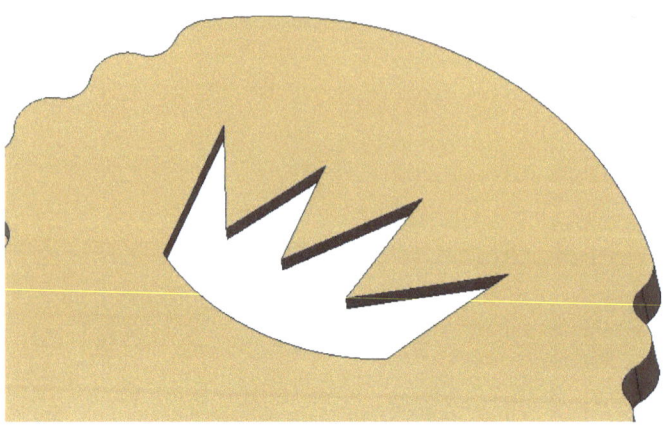

In the round tool, hover over one edge, then tap the RMB (query select) until "IntentEdg" shows. Now click the LMB to select those Intent Edges; you see how all the edges of the crown highlight at once, without having to go around and click on each individual edge.

The completed feature has a round on all the vertical edges.

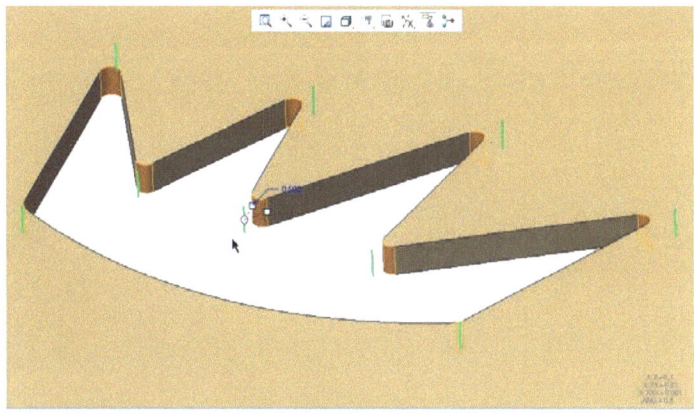

Now, let's say the shape of the crown has to change. We will flatten off some of the points in the sketch.

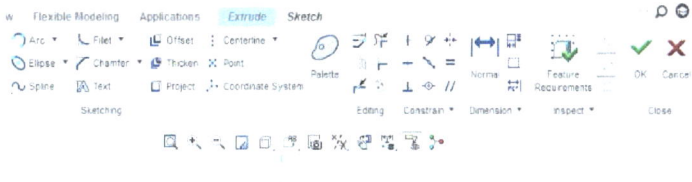

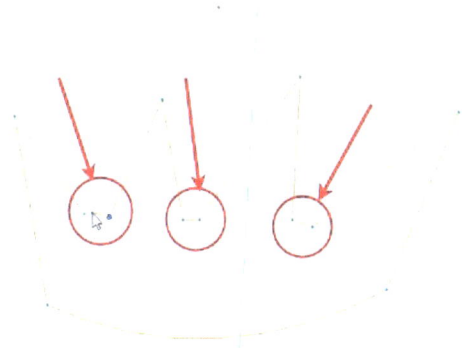

All the rounds will regenerate, even though some of the individual edges are missing. This is a powerful tool.

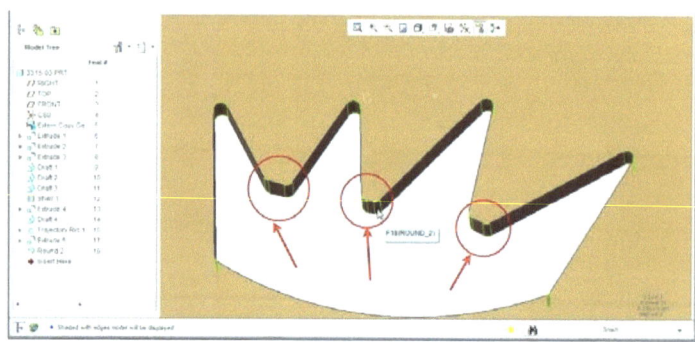

Let's look at another example of Intent Edges. Here we would like to chamfer the four mounting holes. Initiate the Chamfer tool and then Query Select one of the edges until the Intent Edges (all four hole edges) are highlighted. Tap the RMB to make the selection.

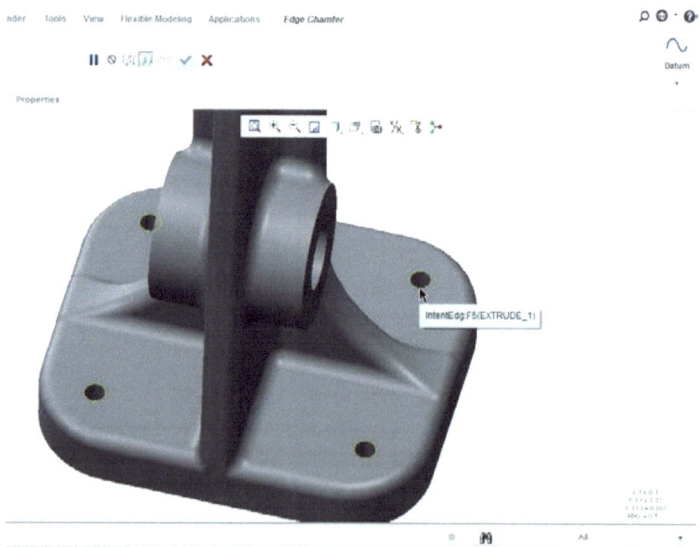

From this one selection, we can chamfer all four holes:

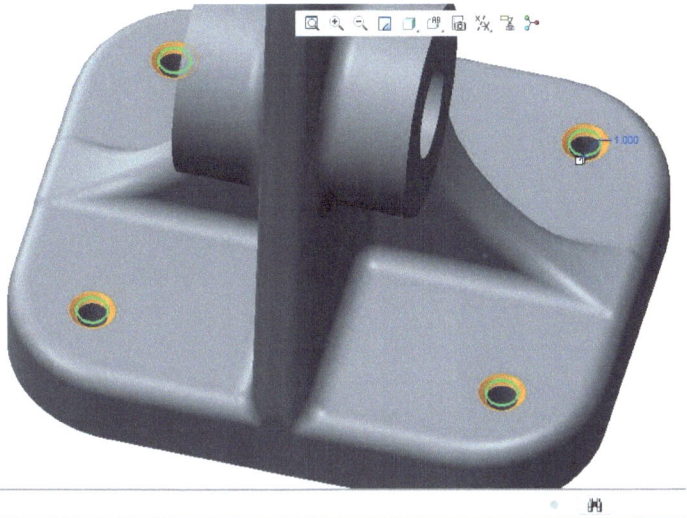

Intent Surfaces:

You can select **Intent Surfaces** in a similar way. This can be useful when drafting multiple faces of a feature. Again, it is a robust selection method, because the geometry can change without causing the draft references to fail.

We want to draft the surfaces of the star. Choose the Draft command. See the following figure:

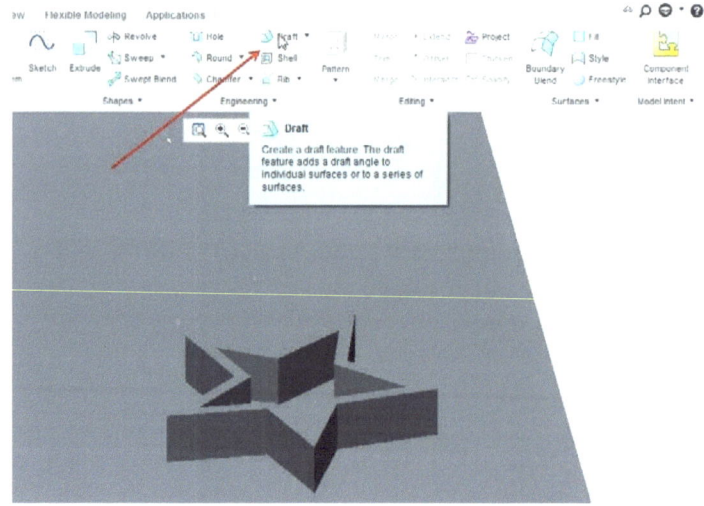

Now, Query Select one of the surfaces of the star until you can choose the Intent Surface:

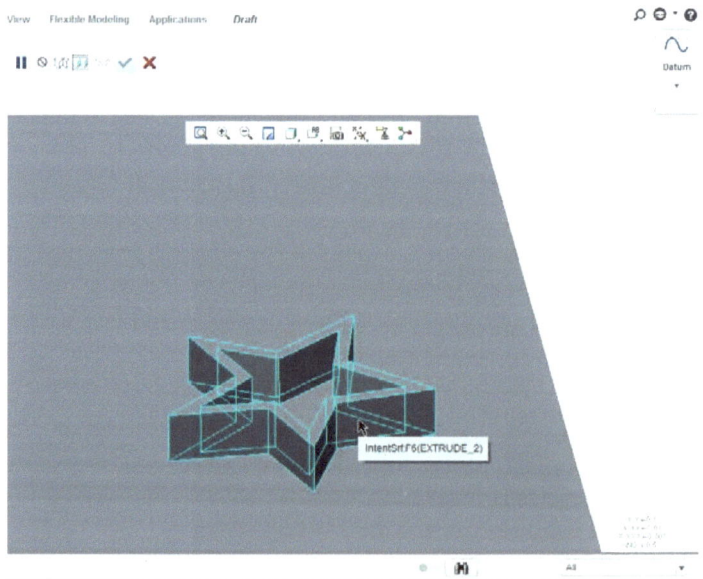

LMB click to make the selection and it will look like this:

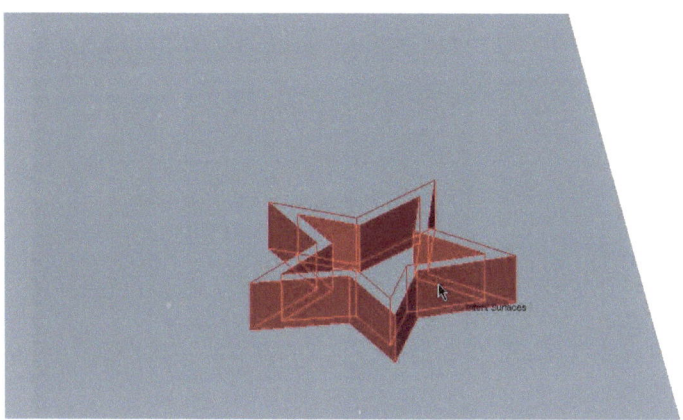

Complete the command and we can see that all the star surfaces are drafted:

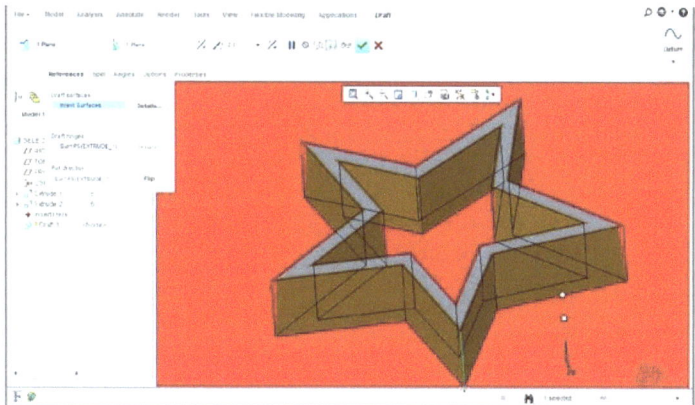

If the shape of the star changes, the draft feature references will update without failing. In fact, the shape could change completely and the draft would still regenerate successfully. Here, we change the sketch of the extrusion to a circle. The draft feature updates now to the surfaces of the circle:

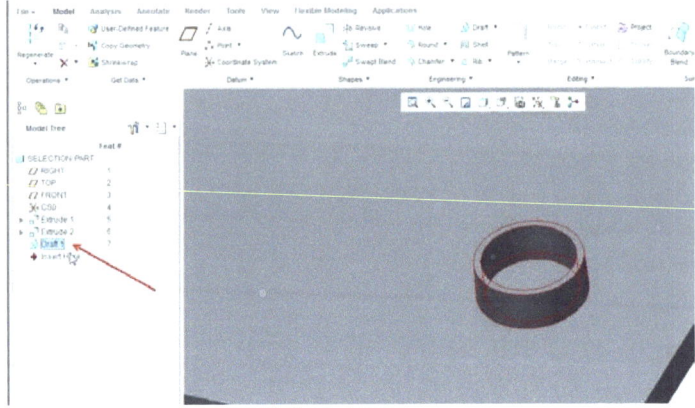

Drawings:

When making a drawing, Creo automatically activates certain selection filters based on what tab (Layout, Table, Annotate, etc...) you have selected. You can overcome the selection filter by holding the ALT key while you click.

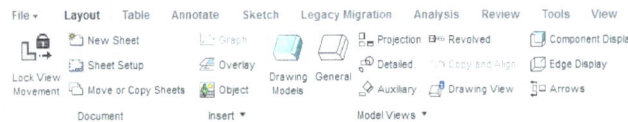

Drawings—Placing Dimensions:

Place dimensions in a drawing using the same click, click, middle click sequence as in sketches. In the drawing you also have some other options if you need more control over how the dimension is placed. The dimension selection defaults to **Select an Entity** selection, which works most of the time.

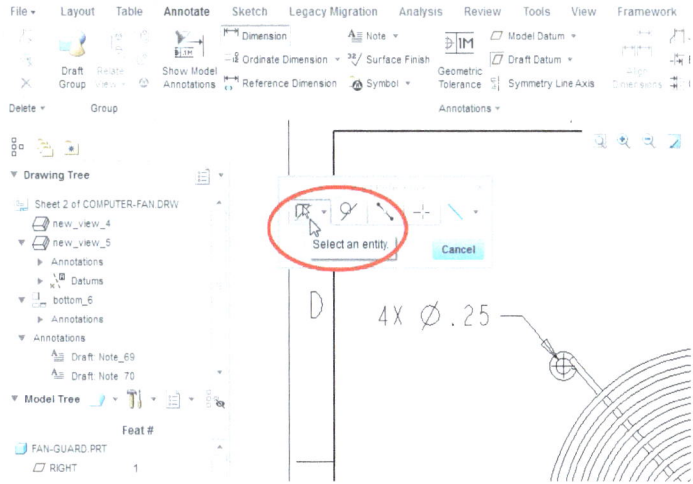

Another useful option is **Intersect**, which allows you to select a point at the intersection of two entities. Hold the CTRL key and select two entities; the drawing will show a highlighted point. See the following figure:

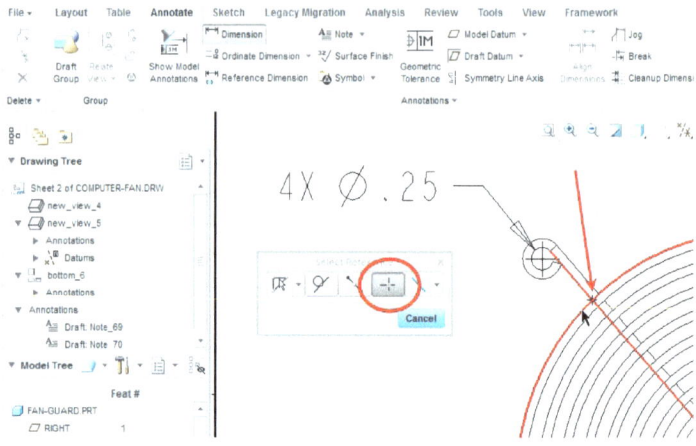

Continue by selecting two more entities while holding the control key; then you will see a preview of the dimension.

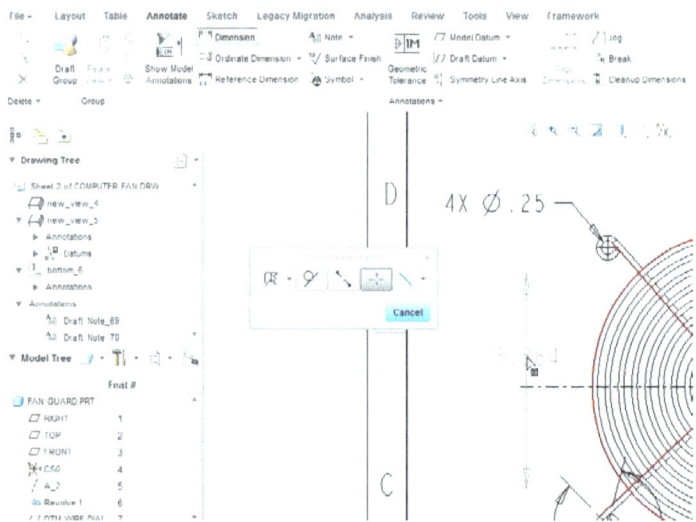

You may hold down the RMB for options on how to place the dimension. In this case choose "Vertical":

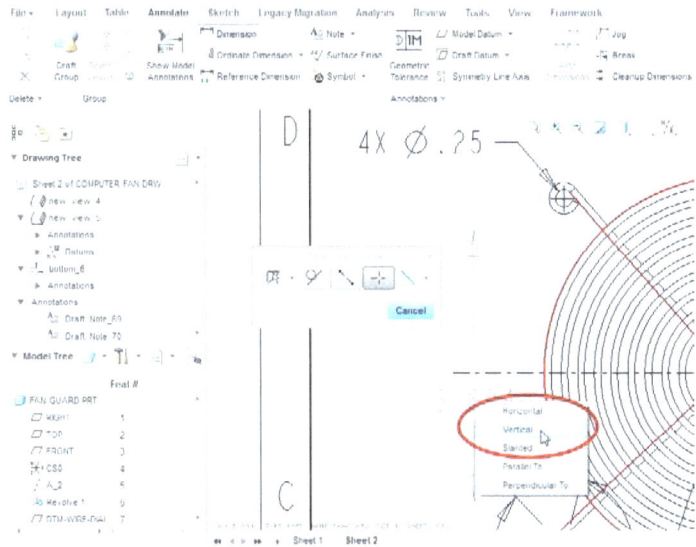

The resulting dimension looks like this:

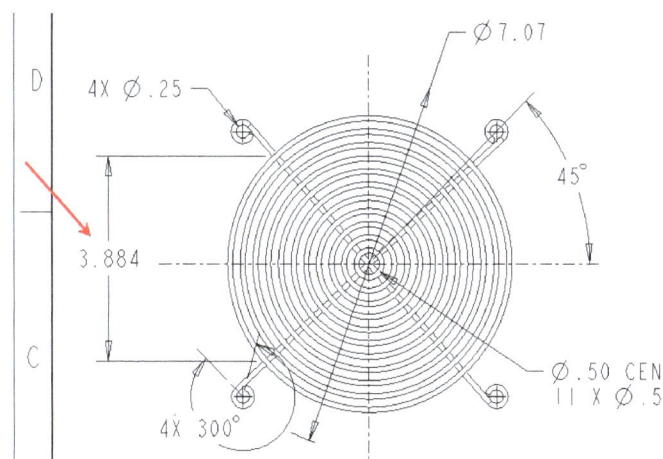

Drawings—Moving Dimensions and Dimension Text:

Select a dimension with the LMB and then you can move it around. While moving a dimension, you can tap the RMB to toggle the arrows into different positions. For instance, you can put the arrows for a diameter dimension inside or outside the circle with the RMB. You can also flip the arrows by accessing the shortcut menu with the RMB. Remember, to get the menu, you must *hold* the RMB, not *tap* it. Under some circumstances tapping the RMB will bring up an alternate shortcut menu.

To move dimension text side-to-side, LMB click the dimension, hold the Shift key, then use the LMB to drag it to the side. This picture shows the dragging arrow you get when you hold the Shift key:

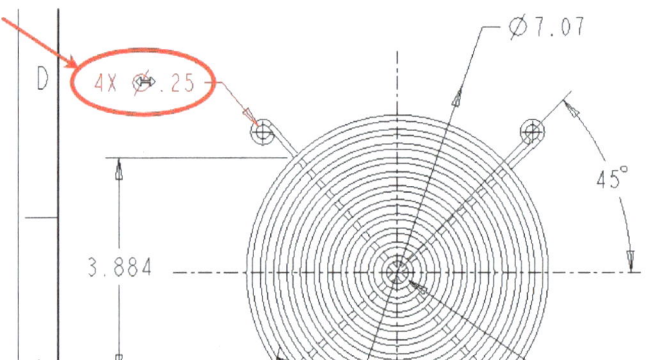

Drag the text to the new position with the LMB:

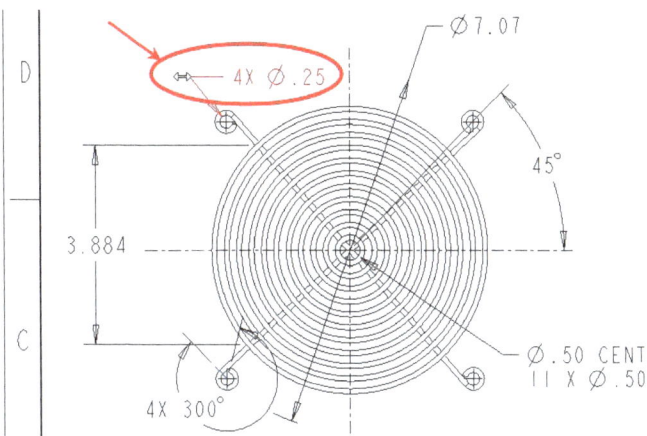

You can also drag the text to the side by *holding* the RMB to access the shortcut menu and choosing **Flip Text**.

Drawings—Properties for Multiple Views

You can change the properties for multiple views all at once. For instance, you could change the display style to "No Hidden" one time and apply it to all selected views. To do this, hold the CTRL key while you LMB click on each of the views. Then hold the RMB to bring up the shortcut menu, and release the button over the selection "Properties".   Whatever changes you make will apply to all the views you selected. See the following figure:

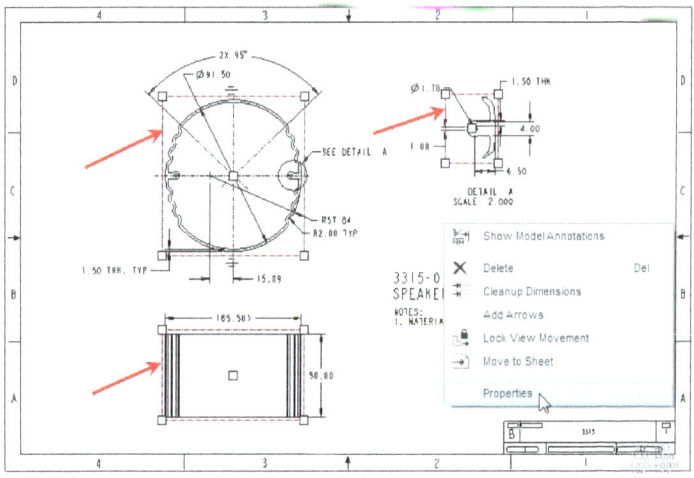

Drawings—Decimal Places Selection

You can change the number of decimal places for a single dimension, for all dimensions, or for just all *new* dimensions that you place. To change the decimal places for a single dimension, double LMB click on it to bring up the Properties box, and change the decimal places there.

To change the default decimal places for all new dimensions expand the "Format" header and choose **Decimal Places**. This setting will not apply to previously placed dimensions.

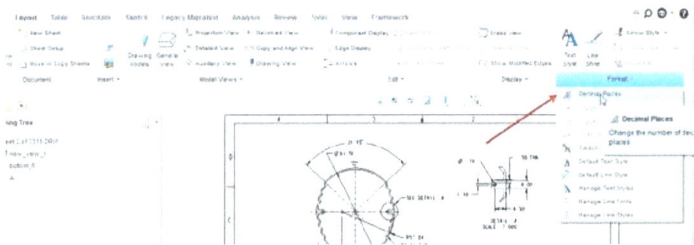

To change the decimal places for all current *and* future dimensions, first drag a box around all existing dimensions with the LMB, then change the decimal places as above using the format menu.

Drawings—Scale

To change the scale for individual views, double LMB click on the view to bring up the "Properties" box and change to a custom scale there. To set the default **Global Scale** for a drawing, double LMB click the scale in the lower left-hand corner and change it:

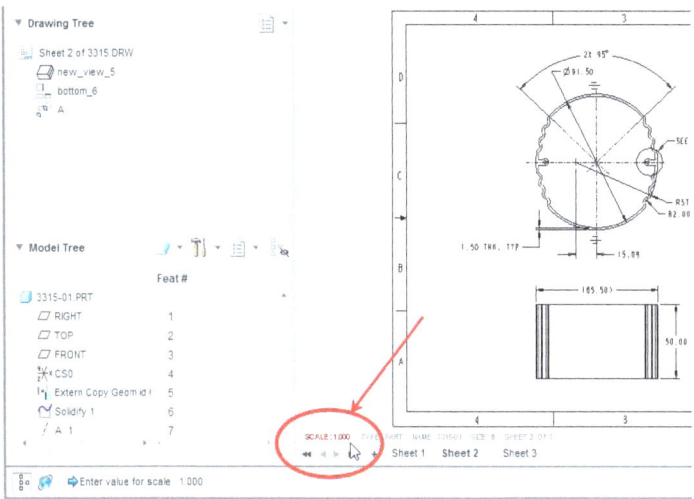

Drawings—Select and Modify Tables and BOM Balloons

You can change the size of individual cells, columns, or rows in a table. First, make sure you have the "Table" tab selected at the top. Then, carefully hover over the cell (or column or row), and LMB click to make that selection. Then hold down the RMB and choose **Width**, or whatever else you would like to change.

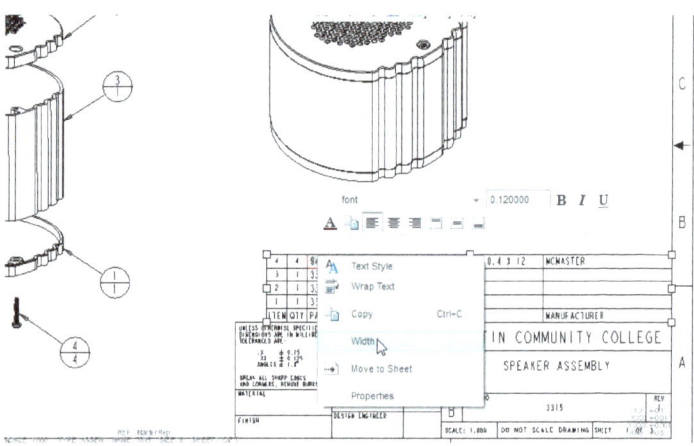

To change the formatting of the entire table, the easiest way to select it is to draw a box around it. Then, hold down the RMB and choose "Properties".

You can LMB click on the BOM balloons to move them around. To change the arrow, first select the balloon with the LBM and then hold the RMB to get a shortcut menu and select **Edit Attachment**. You can now LMB click where you would like the arrow to point. See the following figure:

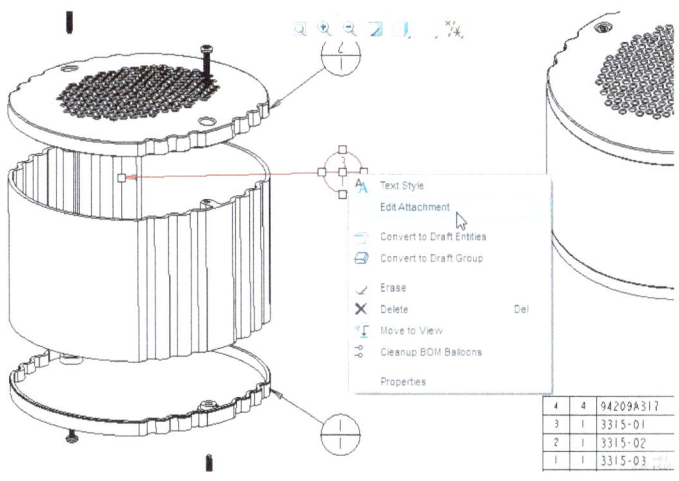

4	4	94209A317
3	1	3315-01
2	1	3315-02
1	1	3315-03

To change the formatting of the balloons, you must select the BOM Table. Crazy, yes, but that is where the formatting options are. Select the whole BOM table by dragging a box around it, then hold the RMB to get the menu and select "Properties". Here you have the option to format the balloons as **Split Balloons** to include the part quantity.

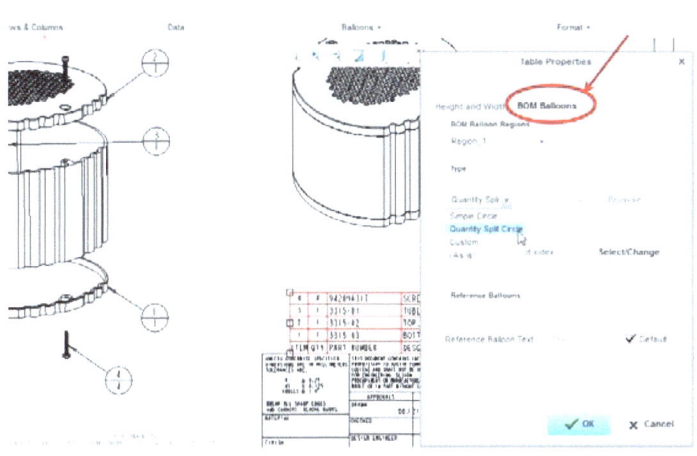

Drawings—Copy/Paste

You may copy and paste notes and other entities from one page to another or even from one drawing to another. First select the note, then type CTRL-C on the keyboard to copy it. Change to another page and then type CTRL-V to paste it. Now you are prompted for some selections. Click in the inset window the attachment point for the existing note; for this one we'll click the upper left-hand edge of the note. Then, in your active drawing click where you would like to paste the note.

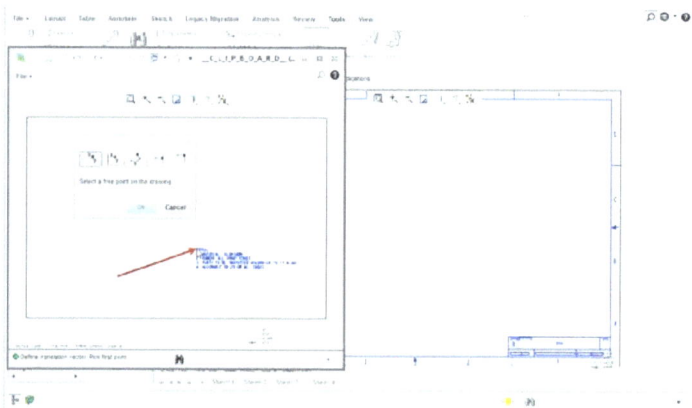

About the Author

Bailey Briscoe Jones (ASME, IDSA) is founder of the product design group, Bright Product Development, and is an adjunct professor of computer aided design at Austin Community College.

www.ingramcontent.com/pod-product-compliance
Lightning Source LLC
Chambersburg PA
CBHW041150050326
40689CB00004B/719